Amazing Animal
Shape-Shifters

by Leon Gray

raintree

C333967814

Raintree is an imprint of Capstone Global Library Limited, a company incorporated in
England and Wales having its registered office at 7 Pilgrim Street, London EC4V 6LB
Registered company number 6695582

www.raintree.co.uk
myorders@raintree.co.uk

Copyright © 2016 Brown Bear Books Ltd

All rights reserved. No part of this publication may be reproduced in whole or in part, or stored
in a retrieval system, or transmitted in any form or by any means, electronic, mechanical, photocopying,
recording, or otherwise, without the prior written permission of the copyright holder.

ISBN: 978-1-4747-0218-8 (HB)
ISBN: 978-1-4747-0224-9

For Brown Bear Books Ltd:
Text: Leon Gray
Editor: Tim Harris
Picture Researcher: Clare Newman
Designer: Karen Perry
Design Manager: Keith Davis
Production Director: Alastair Gourlay
Editorial Director: Lindsey Lowe
Children's Publisher: Anne O'Daly

British Library Cataloguing in Publication Data
A full catalogue record for this book is available from the British Library.

Acknowledgements
Front cover: Cathy Keifer/Shutterstock
1, Cathy Keifer/Shutterstock; 4, Chris T Pehlivan/ Shutterstock; 5tr, Tylinek/Shutterstock; 5bl, Dmitry Rukhlenko/iStock/
Thinkstock; 5bc, Cuson/Shutterstock; 6brs, Paul Reeves Photography /Shutterstock; 6-7background, B. and E. Dudzinscy /
Shutterstock; 6-7, IrinaK/Shutterstock; 7br, Dirk Ercken/Shutterstock; 8, Vitalii Hulai /Shutterstock; 8-9t, manzrussali /Shutterstock;
9b, Anatoliy Lukich/Shutterstock; 11t, Cuson/Shutterstock; 11b, Dirk Ercken /Shutterstock; 12br, Raul Rouzon/National
Geographic Image Collection/Alamy; 12-13, Ken Griffitha/NHPA/Photoshot; 13t, Masahiro Suzuki /Shutterstock; 14, Stubblefield
Photography/Shutterstock; 15t, nicolas.voisin44/Shutterstock; 15b, aquapix/Shutterstock; 16, Alain Compost/Biosphoto/FLPA;
17t, A J Wilhelm/National Geographic Image Collection/Alamy; 17b, David Tipling/Alamy; 18, Andrew Astbury /Shutterstock;
18-19, dibrova /Shutterstock; 19t, Cathy Keifer/Shutterstock; 20, Cathy Keifer/Shutterstock; 21t, Dmitry Rukhlenko/iStock/
Thinkstock; 21b, Cathy Keifer/Shutterstock; 22, J L Klein & M L Hubert/FLPA; 23t, outdoorsman /Shutterstock; 23b, ©Still FX/
Shutterstock; 24, Luke Suen/Shutterstock; 24-25, LFRabanedo/Shutterstock; 25t, Ellen Stenard/iStock/Thinkstock; 26, Nagel
Photography/Shutterstock; 27t, Przemek Tokar/Shutterstock; 27b, Aditya Singh/Getty Images; 28, Michael Stubblefield/Alamy;
29t, Stuart F. Westmorland/Danita Delimont/Alamy; 29b, Ethan Daniels/Alamy.
t=top, c=centre, b=bottom, l=left, r=right

All artworks © Brown Bear Books Ltd
Brown Bear Books has made every attempt to contact the copyright holder.
If anyone has any information please contact licensing@brownbearbooks.co.uk

All the internet addresses (URL's) given in this book were valid at the time of going to press. However, due to the dynamic nature
of the internet some addresses may have changed, or sites may have changed or ceased to exist since publication. While the
copyright holder and publisher regret any inconvenience this may cause readers, no responsibility for any such changes can be
accepted by either the copyright holder or the publisher.

Some words are shown in bold, **like this**. You can find out
what they mean by looking at the glossary.

Printed in China
20 19 18 17 16
10 9 8 7 6 5 4 3 2 1

KU-757-708

Contents

Introduction

The world is full of creatures that change their shape or colour. Some animals change shape as they grow older. Others change their shape or colour to blend in with their surroundings.

When a caterpillar changes shape and turns into a butterfly, this change is called metamorphosis. Other animals make similar changes as they get older. Legless tadpoles become frogs with four legs. Young dragonflies live in water and are wingless. They change into flying insects.

Squid, octopuses and cuttlefish squeeze their bodies into different shapes. They do this to look like pieces of coral or other animals when they are hiding from **predators**.

Other animals change colour. Some male birds lose their feathers in spring. They grow new, brighter feathers to attract female birds. This change usually takes a few weeks. Chameleons can change colour in just a few minutes.

Animals perform the most amazing changes of shape or colour as they grow and to stay safe.

Winter colours

Some creatures change colour with the seasons. Hares, foxes and stoats are brown or grey in the spring or summer. Their fur turns white in winter when snow lies on the ground. They change colour so that they can blend with their surroundings.

Soldiers who train in snowy places wear white clothing and face masks. The soldiers are camouflaged, just like the animals.

COPYCAT

Scientists at the Massachusetts Institute of Technology designed screens wi... inks that v... similar wa... chromato... a chamele...

WOW

South American poison dart frogs release **toxic** chemicals onto their skin. The chemical acts as a defence against predators. Poison dart frogs are usually brightly coloured. Their bright colours warn other animals not to eat them.

Guide for readers

Throughout this book, special feature boxes accompany the main text, captioned photographs and illustrations. COPYCAT boxes highlight some of the ways in which people have been inspired by the animal world. WOW boxes provide incredible facts and figures about different animals.

Metamorphosis

Dogs, cats and horses look like big versions of puppies, kittens and foals. However, some animals go through amazing changes to become adults. These changes are called metamorphosis.

Caterpillars and butterflies

A caterpillar hatches from an egg. It spends all its time eating leaves. As it grows, the caterpillar sheds its skin five or six times. When the caterpillar is ready to become a butterfly, a hard shell, or **pupa**, forms around its body. Inside the pupa, the body of the caterpillar breaks down and new butterfly body parts form. The pupa then splits open and the adult butterfly emerges. The butterfly looks nothing like the pupa or the caterpillar.

Amphibians, such as frogs and salamanders, also go through metamorphosis. So do other animals, such as jellyfish. A jellyfish starts life as a small, swimming **larva**. The larva settles on a rock, and its shape changes. It becomes a **polyp**, which has **tentacles** and catches passing prey. Eventually, parts of the polyp break away and float off into the water. Each part grows into an adult jellyfish.

An adult dragonfly has four wings. Younger dragonflies do not have wings and so cannot fly.

DRAGONFLIES CASE STUDY: PAGE 8

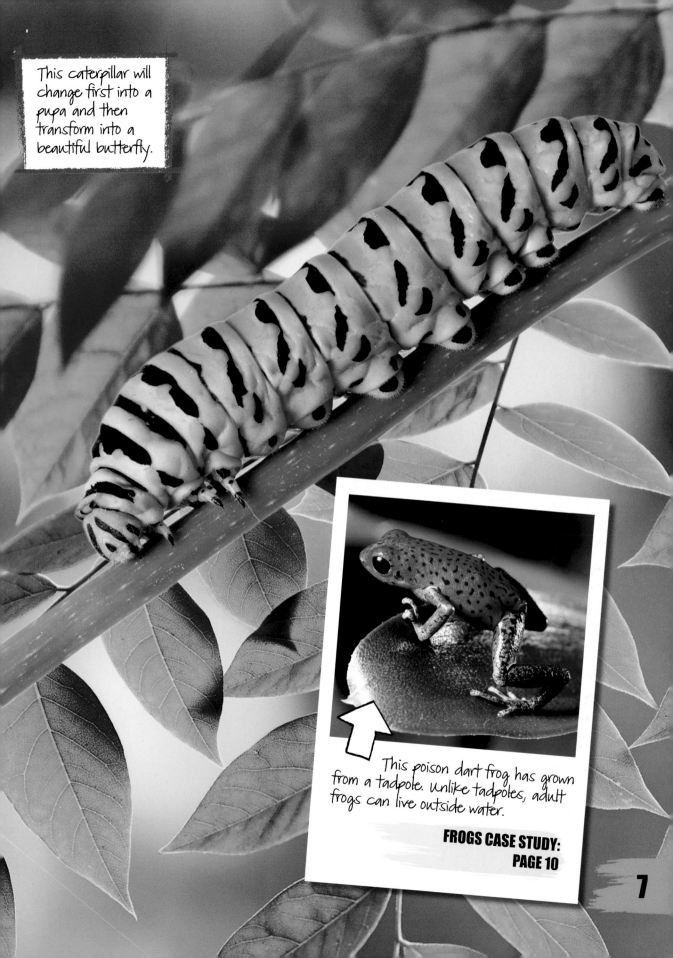

This caterpillar will change first into a pupa and then transform into a beautiful butterfly.

This poison dart frog has grown from a tadpole. Unlike tadpoles, adult frogs can live outside water.

FROGS CASE STUDY:
PAGE 10

7

Dragonflies

Adult dragonflies are flying insects with two pairs of wings and large eyes. These colourful creatures survive for only a few weeks after becoming adults. Before they become adults, dragonflies live underwater.

Dragonfly larvae look nothing like adults. They live and hunt in water.

Living in water

About a week after mating, a female dragonfly lays hundreds of eggs in a stream or lake. A larva hatches from each egg. The young dragonfly larvae are called nymphs. They spend the next couple of years in water. Nymphs breathe using **gills**. They eat as much as they can during this stage in their **life cycle**. The youngest nymphs eat the larvae of other insects. When they get older and bigger the nymphs eat bigger **prey**. Sometimes they even eat small fish.

Most male dragonflies are very colourful. They are often bright yellow, orange or green.

A dragonfly nymph grows in stages. At each stage, the nymph sheds its hard outer covering, or exoskeleton. A new one is underneath. The new exoskeleton is **flexible** for a while. This means the nymph can continue to grow. Each time the nymph sheds its exoskeleton, it grows a little bigger.

Eventually the nymph climbs out of the water. It attaches itself to a plant and puffs up its body with air. The old exoskeleton cracks open and an adult dragonfly squeezes out of it. The dragonfly spreads its wings to dry them. Then it flies away to hunt mosquitoes and other small insects. It will also look for a mate so it can complete its life cycle.

COPYCAT

Dragonflies can fly forwards at up to 56 kilometres (35 miles) per hour. They can also fly backwards, though much more slowly. Just like dragonflies, helicopters can also fly forwards and backwards.

Frogs

Frogs belong to a group of animals called amphibians. Frogs spend several weeks of their lives as tadpoles in ponds or rivers. Slowly, the tadpoles change shape and become adult frogs.

A life in water

There are more than 6,400 different kinds of frogs. They live all over the world. Some live in lakes, rivers and rainforests. Other frogs live in tiny garden ponds. Wherever they live, all frogs need water in which to lay their eggs. Some frogs live in water most of their lives. Others live in dry places much of the year and only visit water when it is time for them to breed.

Tadpoles with long tails emerge from frogspawn. Tadpoles grow four legs and lose their tail as they first become young frogs, then adult frogs.

Life cycle

Like other amphibians, a frog begins life as an egg. A female frog lays thousands of eggs. These float on the surface of the water in clumps called frogspawn. Most of the eggs are eaten by fish, insect larvae, ducks and herons. Only a few survive and hatch into tadpoles.

A tadpole has a long tail but no legs. Like a fish, it has gills to breathe in water. For the first few weeks of its life, a tadpole swims in water. It feeds on **algae** and tries to avoid predators. The tadpole begins to change shape as it grows older. It grows four tiny legs, and lungs form inside its body. At this stage it is called a young frog, or froglet.

The young frog grows bigger. Its mouth becomes wider, its tail gets shorter and its legs grow longer. When its lungs are fully grown, the young frog can begin to breathe air. It is now an adult frog and can leave the water for the first time.

WOW

South American poison dart frogs release **toxic** chemicals onto their skin. The chemical acts as a defence against predators. Poison dart frogs are usually brightly coloured. Their bright colours warn other animals not to eat them.

This adult red-eyed tree frog has feet that are good at clinging to branches.

Changing shape

Some animals have amazing shape-shifting powers when they are fully grown. They can change their shape when they are scared or angry, when they are hiding or when they are attracting mates.

Sizes and shapes

Some lizards spread a frill of skin around their neck when they are threatened. This makes them look more frightening and may scare off a predator.

Animals with soft bodies are the best shape-shifters. They can change the shape of their body more easily than an animal with a bony skeleton. Octopuses escape from predators by squeezing into tiny holes in rocks on the ocean floor.

Male birds often change their shape to attract a mate. Peacocks fan out their colourful tail feathers. Male birds of paradise stretch their wings and spread their tail. Some birds of paradise can change shape until they no longer look like a bird.

A bird of paradise changes its shape when it spreads its wings.

BIRDS OF PARADISE CASE STUDY: PAGE 16

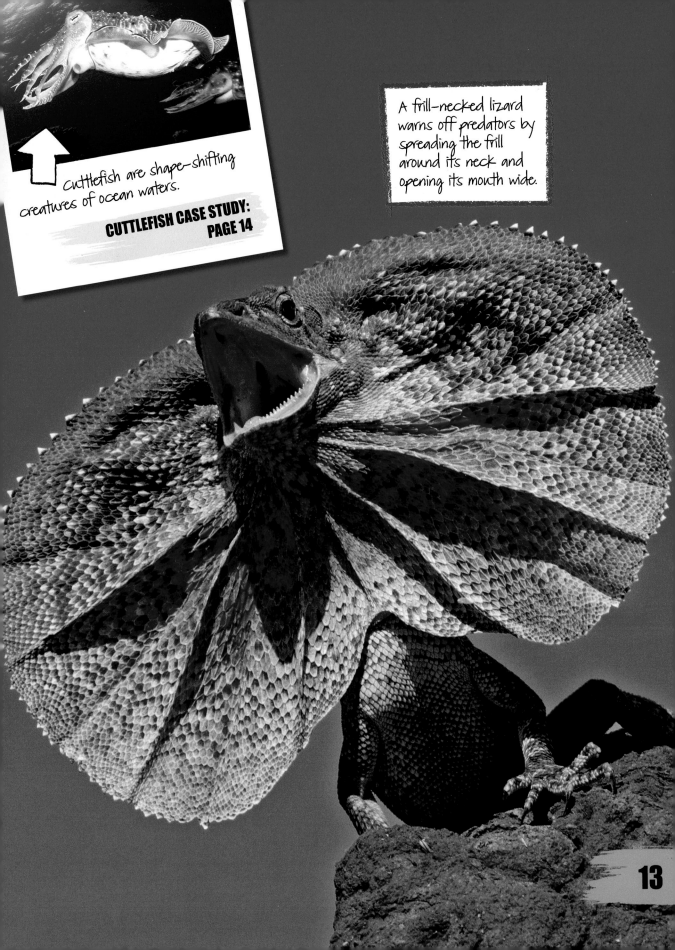

Cuttlefish are shape-shifting creatures of ocean waters.

CUTTLEFISH CASE STUDY:
PAGE 14

A frill-necked lizard warns off predators by spreading the frill around its neck and opening its mouth wide.

Cuttlefish

The cuttlefish is a master of disguise. This ocean creature changes its shape to blend in with its surroundings. The cuttlefish does this to trick its prey and to escape from predators.

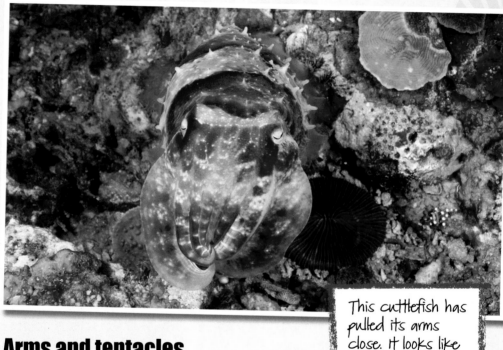

This cuttlefish has pulled its arms close. It looks like part of the seafloor.

Arms and tentacles

Cuttlefish are **molluscs**, not fish. They have large eyes, eight arms and two tentacles covered with suction cups. Most cuttlefish live in shallow water near coral reefs and rocks. They eat crabs and fish, which they grab with their suction cups. It is easy for prey to spot a swimming cuttlefish and escape from it. A hungry cuttlefish has a way around this problem. It disguises itself so that its prey cannot see it. The cuttlefish swims to the seafloor and draws its arms close to its body.

Disguised for hunting

The cuttlefish tightens bands of muscles under its skin. The muscles squeeze its body into different shapes so it looks like part of the seafloor. It remains still until a fish or crab comes close. Then it grabs its victim. A cuttlefish disguises itself in the same way when it is hiding from a predator, such as a seal or shark.

Cuttlefish can also quickly change the colours and patterns on their skin. They do this by sending nerve signals to cells in their skin that contain colour.

WOW

A baby cuttlefish hatches from an egg. Scientists believe that the animal is born with fully formed eyes. That means that a cuttlefish can see while still inside the egg.

The arms of a cuttlefish hang down in front of it when the creature swims.

Birds of paradise

Male birds of paradise use dazzling courtship displays to attract females. They fan out their colourful feathers into different shapes. Often, they do not look like birds at all.

This greater bird of paradise is fanning its tail. The bird looks bigger and brighter and more attractive to mates.

In the forest

Most birds use **courtship** to attract mates in the breeding season. Many male birds whistle songs to draw attention to themselves. Others grow brighter feathers to attract females. Birds of paradise are colourful birds that live on the **tropical** island of New Guinea and in parts of Australia. They live in forests and eat insects and ripe fruits. Male birds of paradise fluff out their feathers during their dramatic courtship displays. They also make clicking noises by moving their wings very fast.

A shape-shifting blue and black male bird of paradise displays its feathers to a female bird.

Most birds of paradise have dark feathers over most of the body. There are a few brighter feathers on the neck, sides, wings and tail. During courtship, male Victoria riflebirds fan out their wings and dark breast feathers. They change their body into an oval shape.

Birds of paradise called parotias perform a different kind of shape-shift. Male parotias change their feathers into the shape of a skirt. They perform a "ballerina dance" to attract females that might be watching from a higher branch.

WOW

In New Guinea, some people use the colourful feathers of birds of paradise for their own displays. People decorate ceremonial headdresses with the feathers. Some birds of paradise are now protected so their feathers cannot be taken.

Colour change

Many animals change colour. Some can change colour in a flash. Others change more slowly. Most animals that change colour do so to help them blend in with their surroundings. Others change to attract a mate or to communicate with each other.

Reasons to change

Chameleons, cuttlefish and jellyfish can change colour quickly so that they match their surroundings. Slug-like sea creatures called nudibranchs change colour when danger threatens. They do this to warn predators that they taste bad.

Other animals change colour more slowly. Some birds **moult** their old feathers and grow bright new ones at the start of the breeding season. They do this to attract mates. For other animals, the changing seasons produce big changes in their habitat. When snow covers the land in winter, Arctic foxes and hares, stoats and birds called ptarmigans lose their brown fur and feathers and turn white to match their surroundings.

Some animals change colour if they are unhealthy. A healthy flamingo is bright pink because of chemicals in the shrimp and algae it eats. If the flamingo's food lacks these chemicals, the flamingo will turn pale pink or white.

An Arctic fox becomes white in winter to match the snow.

ARCTIC FOXES CASE STUDY: PAGE 22

When threatened, chameleons can change colour in a few minutes.

CHAMELEONS CASE STUDY:
PAGE 20

CHAMELEONS CASE STUDY: PAGE 20

The bright colour of these flamingos shows that they are eating a healthy diet.

19

Chameleons

The most amazing thing about chameleons is their incredible colour-changing ability. These creatures change colour to attract a mate and to hide from predators.

This chameleon has caught a fly on the end of its tongue.

Life in the trees

Chameleons are **reptiles** that live in warm regions of the world. Their strong toes and sharp claws help them grip narrow branches as they climb around in trees. When a chameleon spots an insect to eat, it shoots out its long, sticky tongue. The tongue quickly snaps back into the chameleon's mouth, taking the prey with it.

The skin of chameleons is full of special cells called **chromatophores**. These can turn the animal's skin red, yellow, green, blue, purple and pink.

This brightly colou mate chameleon is showing off its colours to a female

If a chameleon's mood changes, the chromatophores change colour. A chameleon becomes darker if it feels threatened. A male may turn bright pink or turquoise to attract a female. A chameleon will turn green to blend in with its forest habitat to hide from predators.

Chameleons are cold-blooded animals. Their body temperature depends on the temperature of their surroundings. Their skin is dark early in the day. Dark colours **absorb** heat better than light colours. This helps the chameleons warm up.

COPYCAT

Scientists at the Massachusetts Institute of Technology designed screens with electronic inks that work in a similar way to the chromatophores in a chameleon's skin.

Arctic foxes

The Arctic is the most northern part of Earth. In winter the land is covered with ice and snow, and the ocean freezes over. The temperature may drop to – 46°C (–50°F). The Arctic fox is one of the few animals that can survive the bitter cold.

This Arctic fox is hunting for prey in summer.

Surviving the cold

The Arctic fox is a tough predator. It has a layer of fat around its body. The fat keeps its heart and other **internal** organs warm even in the middle of winter. The fox's body is covered with thick fur. So is its tail. Even its paws are furry.

The Arctic is not always frozen. In spring the weather is warmer. The brown and grey rocks beneath the snow appear as the snow melts. This is when Arctic foxes hunt for food and raise cubs. The foxes have brown and grey fur, so they are a similar colour to their surroundings.

In autumn, snow covers the ground. The Arctic foxes moult their brown and grey fur and grow brilliant white fur. It is hard to see a white fox walking on white snow and ice. This makes it harder for birds, hares, lemmings and other prey to see them. The foxes can catch their prey more easily.

A fox uses its keen sense of hearing to find prey under the snow. When it hears a faint movement, the fox strikes through the snow to catch its food.

COPYCAT

Long ago people hunted Arctic foxes. They killed thousands of them for their fur. The fur was made into coats to keep people warm. Not as many people wear real fur coats now, which is one reason why the number of Arctic foxes has increased.

In winter, the Arctic fox's white coat blends in with the snow.

Camouflage

Some animals have colours, patterns or shapes that help them blend in with their surroundings. This is called camouflage. It helps prey animals hide from predators. It helps predators hunt for prey without being seen.

Colors, patterns and shapes

Many animals have colours and patterns that are the same as their background. Polar bears are white to blend in with snow and ice. Desert animals such as camels are often light brown to make it hard to see them in the desert.

Other animals have patterns that break up their body shape. This makes it more difficult to see them. The spotted coat of a leopard blends in with its grassland habitat. The stripes of a tiger's fur make the big cat harder to see in forests.

Shape is another kind of camouflage. Some animals hide from predators by looking like a different object. Stick insects look just like sticks, while planthoppers are shaped like leaves.

Some animals copy the patterns and colours of another creature that is dangerous. This is called mimicry. A harmless animal is more likely to survive if predators think it is dangerous.

A mimic octopus has made itself look like a starfish to avoid being eaten

MIMIC OCTOPUSES CASE STUDY: PAGE 28

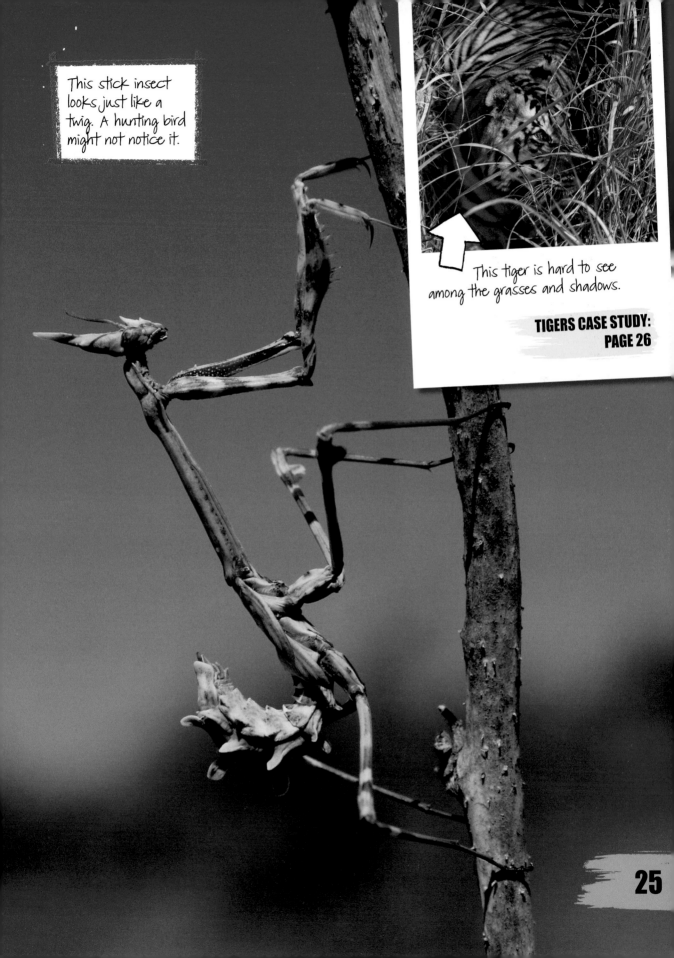

This stick insect looks just like a twig. A hunting bird might not notice it.

This tiger is hard to see among the grasses and shadows.

TIGERS CASE STUDY: PAGE 26

Tigers

Tigers are the biggest members of the cat family. They are fearsome predators. A tiger's fur is orange with black stripes. The stripes on a tiger's fur help it hide from its prey when it is hunting. No two tigers have exactly the same pattern of stripes.

Ambush predators

Tigers are ambush predators. This means they pounce on their prey without warning. Most tigers live in forests but some live in grasslands. The striped fur of the tiger provides excellent camouflage in these **habitats**.

Tigers that live in snowy Siberia have paler colours than tigers that live in hot, sunny forests.

A hungry tiger listens for the sound of a deer, pig or cow moving. The tiger moves slowly and quietly to get closer to its prey. When it is close enough it leaps onto the victim and kills it. Tigers are so powerful that they can kill animals larger than themselves.

Tigers in cold lands

Most tigers live in warm parts of the world such as India, Thailand, Malaysia and Indonesia. Snow is rare in those places. Some tigers live in colder places, though. Amur tigers live in eastern Siberia, where snow covers the ground in winter. These tigers have slightly paler fur. However, their orange and black fur does not completely camouflage them when they are in open areas covered by snow.

COPYCAT

Soldiers fighting in forests wear green or brown camouflage clothing. This keeps them hidden as they move between the trees. Soldiers sometimes wear camouflage nets. They even put camouflage colours on their helmets and guns.

This tiger's stripes help it blend in with its forest surroundings.

Mimic octopuses

The mimic octopus swims in shallow ocean waters around South-east Asia. For much of the time this octopus remains hidden and camouflaged among rocks on the seafloor.

Like other octopuses, this creature is a predator. It hunts fish and crabs. When it is hungry, a mimic octopus leaves its hiding place on the seafloor. It swoops through the water and grasps its prey with its tentacles. Then the octopus draws the victim into its mouth.

A mimic octopus rests on the seafloor. This is how it looks when it is not copying another creature.

Colour changers

Most octopuses can change their skin colour to match their surroundings. A mimic octopus can disguise itself even better than other octopuses. It changes colour and twists and folds its body into shapes that look like other sea creatures.

Different disguises

The mimic octopus can disguise itself as a dangerous animal such as a lionfish, a flounder fish or a sea snake. If a predator thinks the octopus is more dangerous than it really is, the hunting animal will leave it alone.

A mimic octopus can also change to look like a starfish. This is not a dangerous animal, but it is tough to eat. A hungry predator might decide not to eat it.

This mimic octopus has arranged its arms so it looks like a flounder fish.

WOW

Octopuses have another way to defend themselves from predators. When they feel threatened, these creatures squirt a jet of blue-black ink from a sac inside their body. The octopus then makes its escape behind a cloud of ink that spreads through the water.

Glossary

absorb soak up

algae plantlike life forms

amphibians cold-blooded animals such as frogs and salamanders that spend part of their life in water and part of their life on land

chromatophores cells containing chemicals called pigments. These allow an animal to change colour

courtship way in which animals attract other animals to mate and produce offspring

flexible bendable

gills body parts that allow fish and young frogs to breathe in water

habitats natural homes of animals or plants

internal on the inside of the body

larva young form of an animal such as an insect, jellyfish or amphibian

life cycle stages through which a living thing passes from the start of its life until its death

molluscs soft-bodied animals such as cuttlefish and octopuses

moult when one set of skin, fur or feathers is replaced by a new set

polyp stage in the life cycle of a jellyfish between the planula and the adult form

predators animals that hunt and eat other animals

prey animal that is hunted and eaten by other animals

pupa stage in the life cycle of most insects when the larva changes into the adult form

reptiles cold-blooded animals with scaly skin, such as lizards or snakes

tentacles long, flexible arms of an animal such as an octopus

toxic containing poisonous substances

tropical warm regions to the north and south of the Equator

Read more

Amazing Animal Life Cycles (Wow! Wildlife), Alix Wood (Windmill Books, 2012).

Animals that Hide (Adapted to Survive), Angela Royston (Raintree, 2014).

Birds (Really Weird Animals), Clare Hibbert (Hachette, 2015).

Butterflies and Moths (Really Weird Animals), Clare Hibbert (Hachette, 2015).

Focus on Amphibians (Classification), Stephen Savage (Wayland, 2014).

Focus on Insects (Classification), Stephen Savage (Wayland, 2014).

Internet sites

Animal fact guide
This page looks at how octopuses change colour.
www.animalfactguide.com/animal-facts/common-octopus

Learn about nature
Information about butterfly metamorphosis with lots of pictures.
www.thebutterflysite.com/life-cycle.shtml

The Learning Zone
The Oxford University children's learning zone looks at the ways different animals change as they grow.
www.oum.ox.ac.uk/thezone/animals/life/grow.htm

Index